C000050373

This book belongs to

....

....

Mike was eating his dinner,
but carrots he didn't like.

So he passed them slyly to Monty, who gulped them down in one **BITE!**

BURP!

Mom asked,

"Did you feed those to Monty?"

Mike and Monty were playing chase in the house when Mike knocked a vase off the shelf.

It *SMASHED* into pieces when it hit the floor, but Mike didn't own up himself.

One day, they were throwing balls through the hoop while they played in the yard.

Mike kept his monkey, and they still have fun,
but now Mike says, "Sorry, it was me."

THANK YOU

I read and appreciate all of feedback and reviews, it would mean the world to me if you would leave a review on Amazon – this would help support me to create more wonderful children's books!

About the Author

Sadie Gardner is a children's book author from London. She prides herself on creating stories with valuable lessons and message within them.

Follow me on

Instagram: Sadiegardnerbooks

Facebook: https://fb.me/sadiegardnerbooks

Twitter: https://twitter.com/SadieGardbooks

Free Gift!

Scan me to recieve your free copy!

Make sure you download your free 'Mike And His Pet Monkey Activity Book'!

Simply open up your camera on your smart phone, hover over the QR code and click the banner that appears to leave a review!

Printed in Poland
by Amazon Fulfillment
Poland Sp. z o.o., Wrocław

64783192R00019